This Crochet Planner
Belongs to

-------------------------------------------------------------

-------------------------------------------------------------

-------------------------------------------------------------

# VISIT OUR WEBSITE

Learn more about our mission and find our latest updates, hot new releases, freebies, and more.
www.thebubble.press

DON'T FORGET TO RATE THE PRODUCT AND LEAVE A COMMENT.

We care about your opinion!
Help us improve our products.

## The Bubble Press
### Your Dedicated Partner

Copyright © 2020

# Table of Contents

# Table of Contents

# Table of Contents

# Table of Contents

# Table of Contents

# Table of Contents

# Table of Contents

# Table of Contents

Crochet

Keeps My Hands Busy

My Mind Calm

My Heart Happy

**01** Project Name .....................................................................

For ..................................... Occasion .....................................

Start Date ........................... End Date .....................................

Pattern ..............................................................................

Design Source .......................................................................

Yarn ................................................................................

Color / dye lot .....................................................................

.....................................................................................

Weight ..............................................................................

WPI .................................................................................

Fiber ...............................................................................

Hook Size ...........................................................................

Gauge ...............................................................................

Washing Instructions
.....................................................................................
.....................................................................................
.....................................................................................
.....................................................................................
.....................................................................................
.....................................................................................

Notes ...............................................................................
.....................................................................................
.....................................................................................
.....................................................................................

Rating ☆ ☆ ☆ ☆ ☆          Difficulty ▢ ▢ ▢ ▢ ▢ ▢

Sketch ✂

**02** Project Name ...........................................................................

For ............................................ Occasion ..........................................

Start Date .................................... End Date ..........................................

Pattern ..............................................................................................

Design Source ......................................................................................

Yarn ...............................................................

Color / dye lot ...............................................

...........................................................................

Weight ...........................................................

WPI ................................................................

Fiber ..............................................................

Hook Size ......................................................

Gauge ............................................................

Washing Instructions

...........................................................................

...........................................................................

...........................................................................

...........................................................................

...........................................................................

...........................................................................

...........................................................................

Notes ................................................................................................

...........................................................................................................

...........................................................................................................

...........................................................................................................

...........................................................................................................

Rating ☆ ☆ ☆ ☆ ☆          Difficulty ☐ ☐ ☐ ☐ ☐ ☐

Sketch ✂

**03** Project Name ..............................................

For ............................  Occasion ............................

Start Date ....................  End Date ............................

Pattern .......................................................

Design Source .................................................

Yarn ..........................................................

Color / dye lot ...............................................

..............................................................

Weight ........................................................

WPI ...........................................................

Fiber .........................................................

Hook Size .....................................................

Gauge .........................................................

Washing Instructions
..............................................................
..............................................................
..............................................................
..............................................................
..............................................................

Notes .........................................................
..............................................................
..............................................................
..............................................................
..............................................................

Rating ☆ ☆ ☆ ☆ ☆    Difficulty ☐ ☐ ☐ ☐ ☐ ☐

Sketch ✂

**04** Project Name .................................................

For .................................. Occasion ..................................

Start Date .............................. End Date ..............................

Pattern ..................................................................

Design Source ..........................................................

Yarn ..................................................

Color / dye lot ......................................

..................................................................

Weight ..................................................

WPI ..................................................

Fiber ..................................................

Hook Size ..........................................

Gauge ..................................................

Washing Instructions
..................................................
..................................................
..................................................
..................................................
..................................................
..................................................
..................................................
..................................................

Notes ..................................................................
..................................................................
..................................................................
..................................................................
..................................................................

Rating ☆ ☆ ☆ ☆ ☆          Difficulty ▢ ▢ ▢ ▢ ▢ ▢

Sketch ✂

**05** Project Name _____

For _____ Occasion _____

Start Date _____ End Date _____

Pattern _____

Design Source _____

Yarn _____

Color / dye lot _____

_____

Weight _____

WPI _____

Fiber _____

Hook Size _____

Gauge _____

Washing Instructions

_____

_____

_____

_____

_____

_____

Notes _____

_____

_____

_____

Rating ☆ ☆ ☆ ☆ ☆          Difficulty ☐ ☐ ☐ ☐ ☐ ☐

18

Sketch ✂

**06** Project Name ...........................................................................................................................

For ........................................................... Occasion ...........................................................

Start Date ........................................... End Date ...........................................

Pattern ...........................................................................................................................

Design Source ...........................................................................................................

Yarn ...........................................................................................

Color / dye lot ...........................................................................

...........................................................................................................

Weight ...........................................................................................

WPI ...........................................................................................

Fiber ...........................................................................................

Hook Size ...........................................................................

Gauge ...........................................................................

Washing Instructions

...........................................................................

...........................................................................

...........................................................................

...........................................................................

...........................................................................

...........................................................................

...........................................................................

Notes ...........................................................................................................................

...........................................................................................................................

...........................................................................................................................

...........................................................................................................................

...........................................................................................................................

Rating ☆ ☆ ☆ ☆ ☆          Difficulty ☐ ☐ ☐ ☐ ☐ ☐

Sketch ✂

**07** Project Name .................................................

For ........................... Occasion ...........................

Start Date ..................... End Date ...........................

Pattern .............................................................

Design Source .......................................................

Yarn ................................................

Color / dye lot .....................................

.....................................................

Weight ..............................................

WPI .................................................

Fiber ...............................................

Hook Size ...........................................

Gauge ...............................................

Washing Instructions
.....................................
.....................................
.....................................
.....................................
.....................................
.....................................
.....................................

Notes ...............................................................
.....................................................................
.....................................................................
.....................................................................
.....................................................................

Rating ☆ ☆ ☆ ☆ ☆          Difficulty ☐ ☐ ☐ ☐ ☐

Sketch ✂

## 08 Project Name

For _____  Occasion _____

Start Date _____  End Date _____

Pattern _____

Design Source _____

Yarn _____

Color / dye lot _____

_____

Weight _____

WPI _____

Fiber _____

Hook Size _____

Gauge _____

Washing Instructions

_____

_____

_____

_____

_____

_____

Notes _____

_____

_____

_____

Rating ☆ ☆ ☆ ☆ ☆    Difficulty ☐ ☐ ☐ ☐ ☐

Sketch ✂

**09** Project Name ...................................................

For .......................................... Occasion ..........................................

Start Date .......................................... End Date ..........................................

Pattern ..........................................

Design Source ..........................................

Yarn ..........................................

Color / dye lot ..........................................

..........................................

Weight ..........................................

WPI ..........................................

Fiber ..........................................

Hook Size ..........................................

Gauge ..........................................

Washing Instructions

..........................................

..........................................

..........................................

..........................................

..........................................

..........................................

Notes ..........................................

..........................................

..........................................

..........................................

..........................................

Rating ☆ ☆ ☆ ☆ ☆ Difficulty ☐ ☐ ☐ ☐ ☐

Sketch ✂

**10** Project Name ........................................................................

For ........................................ Occasion ........................................

Start Date ................................ End Date ................................

Pattern ........................................................................

Design Source ........................................................................

Yarn ........................................................................

Color / dye lot ........................................................................

........................................................................

Weight ........................................................................

WPI ........................................................................

Fiber ........................................................................

Hook Size ........................................................................

Gauge ........................................................................

Washing Instructions

........................................................................

........................................................................

........................................................................

........................................................................

........................................................................

........................................................................

Notes ........................................................................

........................................................................

........................................................................

........................................................................

Rating ☆ ☆ ☆ ☆ ☆          Difficulty ▢ ▢ ▢ ▢ ▢ ▢

Sketch ✂

**11** Project Name _____

For _____  Occasion _____

Start Date _____  End Date _____

Pattern _____

Design Source _____

Yarn _____

Color / dye lot _____

_____

Weight _____

WPI _____

Fiber _____

Hook Size _____

Gauge _____

Washing Instructions

_____

_____

_____

_____

_____

Notes _____

_____

_____

_____

_____

Rating ☆ ☆ ☆ ☆ ☆   Difficulty ☐ ☐ ☐ ☐ ☐ ☐

Sketch ✂

**12** Project Name _____

For _____ Occasion _____

Start Date _____ End Date _____

Pattern _____

Design Source _____

Yarn _____

Color / dye lot _____

_____

Weight _____

WPI _____

Fiber _____

Hook Size _____

Gauge _____

Washing Instructions

_____

_____

_____

_____

_____

_____

Notes _____

_____

_____

_____

Rating ☆ ☆ ☆ ☆ ☆          Difficulty ☐ ☐ ☐ ☐ ☐ ☐

Sketch ✂

**13** Project Name ................................................................................

For ...................................... Occasion ......................................

Start Date ...................................... End Date ......................................

Pattern ......................................................................

Design Source ......................................................................

Yarn ......................................................................

Color / dye lot ......................................................................

......................................................................

Weight ......................................................................

WPI ......................................................................

Fiber ......................................................................

Hook Size ......................................................................

Gauge ......................................................................

Washing Instructions

......................................................................

......................................................................

......................................................................

......................................................................

......................................................................

......................................................................

Notes ......................................................................

......................................................................

......................................................................

......................................................................

......................................................................

Rating ☆ ☆ ☆ ☆ ☆ Difficulty ☐ ☐ ☐ ☐ ☐ ☐

Sketch ✂

**14** Project Name .............................................

For ................................ Occasion ................................

Start Date ................................ End Date ................................

Pattern ................................................

Design Source ................................................

Yarn ................................................
Color / dye lot ................................................
................................................

Weight ................................................
WPI ................................................

Fiber ................................................

Hook Size ................................................

Gauge ................................................

Washing Instructions
................................................
................................................
................................................
................................................
................................................
................................................

Notes ................................................
................................................
................................................
................................................
................................................

Rating ☆ ☆ ☆ ☆ ☆        Difficulty ▢ ▢ ▢ ▢ ▢ ▢

Sketch ✄

**15** Project Name ........................................................

For ........................................ Occasion ........................................

Start Date ........................................ End Date ........................................

Pattern ........................................................

Design Source ........................................................

Yarn ........................................................

Color / dye lot ........................................................

........................................................

Weight ........................................................

WPI ........................................................

Fiber ........................................................

Hook Size ........................................................

Gauge ........................................................

Washing Instructions

........................................................

........................................................

........................................................

........................................................

........................................................

........................................................

Notes ........................................................

........................................................

........................................................

........................................................

Rating ☆ ☆ ☆ ☆ ☆   Difficulty ☐ ☐ ☐ ☐ ☐

Sketch

**16** Project Name ........................................

For ........................ Occasion ........................

Start Date ........................ End Date ........................

Pattern ........................................

Design Source ........................................

Yarn ........................................
Color / dye lot ........................................

........................................

Weight ........................................
WPI ........................................
Fiber ........................................

Hook Size ........................................

Gauge ........................................

Washing Instructions
........................................
........................................
........................................
........................................
........................................
........................................

Notes ........................................
........................................
........................................
........................................
........................................

Rating ☆ ☆ ☆ ☆ ☆          Difficulty ☐ ☐ ☐ ☐ ☐ ☐

Sketch ✂

**17** Project Name ........................................................

For ........................................... Occasion ...................................

Start Date ................................. End Date ...................................

Pattern ......................................................................

Design Source ..................................................................

Yarn ..........................................................

Color / dye lot ...............................................

..................................................................

Weight ...........................................................

WPI ..............................................................

Fiber ............................................................

Hook Size ...................................................

Gauge ........................................................

Washing Instructions

..................................................................

..................................................................

..................................................................

..................................................................

..................................................................

..................................................................

Notes ...........................................................................

..................................................................................

..................................................................................

..................................................................................

..................................................................................

Rating ☆ ☆ ☆ ☆ ☆          Difficulty ☐ ☐ ☐ ☐ ☐

Sketch ✂

**18** Project Name .....................................................................................

For ................................................ Occasion ...............................................

Start Date ........................................ End Date ...............................................

Pattern .............................................................................................................

Design Source ................................................................................................

Yarn ...............................................................

Color / dye lot .............................................................

.....................................................................................

Weight .........................................................................

WPI .............................................................................

Fiber ...........................................................................

Hook Size ...................................................................

Gauge ........................................................................

Washing Instructions
.....................................................................................
.....................................................................................
.....................................................................................
.....................................................................................
.....................................................................................

Notes ...............................................................................................................
.............................................................................................................................
.............................................................................................................................
.............................................................................................................................
.............................................................................................................................

Rating ☆ ☆ ☆ ☆ ☆          Difficulty ☐ ☐ ☐ ☐ ☐ ☐

Sketch ✂

**19** Project Name _____

For _____ Occasion _____

Start Date _____ End Date _____

Pattern _____

Design Source _____

Yarn _____

Color / dye lot _____

_____

Weight _____

WPI _____

Fiber _____

Hook Size _____

Gauge _____

Washing Instructions
_____
_____
_____
_____
_____
_____

Notes _____
_____
_____
_____

Rating ☆ ☆ ☆ ☆ ☆          Difficulty ☐ ☐ ☐ ☐ ☐ ☐

Sketch ✂

**20** Project Name ........................................................

For .......................................... Occasion ...........................................

Start Date .......................................... End Date ...........................................

Pattern ...........................................

Design Source ...........................................

Yarn ...........................................

Color / dye lot ...........................................

...........................................

Weight ...........................................

WPI ...........................................

Fiber ...........................................

Hook Size ...........................................

Gauge ...........................................

Washing Instructions

...........................................
...........................................
...........................................
...........................................
...........................................
...........................................
...........................................

Notes ...........................................

...........................................
...........................................
...........................................
...........................................

Rating ☆ ☆ ☆ ☆ ☆        Difficulty ▢ ▢ ▢ ▢ ▢ ▢

Sketch ✂

**21** Project Name ........................................

For ........................................ Occasion ........................................

Start Date ........................................ End Date ........................................

Pattern ........................................

Design Source ........................................

Yarn ........................................

Color / dye lot ........................................

........................................

Weight ........................................

WPI ........................................

Fiber ........................................

Hook Size ........................................

Gauge ........................................

Washing Instructions

........................................

........................................

........................................

........................................

........................................

........................................

Notes ........................................

........................................

........................................

........................................

........................................

Rating ☆ ☆ ☆ ☆ ☆ Difficulty ☐ ☐ ☐ ☐ ☐ ☐

Sketch ✂

**22** Project Name _____

For _____ Occasion _____

Start Date _____ End Date _____

Pattern _____

Design Source _____

Yarn _____

Color / dye lot _____

_____

Weight _____

WPI _____

Fiber _____

Hook Size _____

Gauge _____

Washing Instructions

_____

_____

_____

_____

_____

Notes _____

_____

_____

_____

_____

Rating ☆ ☆ ☆ ☆ ☆    Difficulty ☐ ☐ ☐ ☐ ☐ ☐

Sketch ✂

**23** Project Name ........................................................

For .................................... Occasion ........................................

Start Date .................................... End Date ....................................

Pattern ........................................................

Design Source ........................................................

Yarn ........................................................

Color / dye lot ....................................

........................................................

Weight ....................................

WPI ....................................

Fiber ....................................

Hook Size ....................................

Gauge ....................................

Washing Instructions

........................................................

........................................................

........................................................

........................................................

........................................................

Notes ........................................................

........................................................

........................................................

........................................................

Rating ☆ ☆ ☆ ☆ ☆    Difficulty ☐ ☐ ☐ ☐ ☐ ☐

Sketch ✂

**24** Project Name .................................................

For .................................... Occasion ....................................

Start Date .................................... End Date ....................................

Pattern ....................................................................

Design Source ....................................................................

Yarn ....................................................................
Color / dye lot ....................................................................

....................................................................

Weight ....................................................................
WPS ....................................................................

Fiber ....................................................................

Hook Size ....................................................................

Gauge ....................................................................

Washing Instructions
....................................................................
....................................................................
....................................................................
....................................................................
....................................................................
....................................................................

Notes ....................................................................
....................................................................
....................................................................
....................................................................
....................................................................

Rating ☆ ☆ ☆ ☆ ☆          Difficulty ☐ ☐ ☐ ☐ ☐ ☐

Sketch >&8

**25** Project Name ...........................................................................................

For ........................................... Occasion ...........................................

Start Date ........................................... End Date ...........................................

Pattern ...........................................................................................

Design Source ...........................................................................................

Yarn ...........................................................................................

Color / dye lot ...........................................................................................

...........................................................................................

Weight ...........................................................................................

WPI ...........................................................................................

Fiber ...........................................................................................

Hook Size ...........................................................................................

Gauge ...........................................................................................

Washing Instructions

...........................................................................................

...........................................................................................

...........................................................................................

...........................................................................................

...........................................................................................

...........................................................................................

Notes ...........................................................................................

...........................................................................................

...........................................................................................

...........................................................................................

Rating ☆ ☆ ☆ ☆ ☆          Difficulty ☐ ☐ ☐ ☐ ☐

Sketch ✂

**26** Project Name _____

For _____ Occasion _____

Start Date _____ End Date _____

Pattern _____

Design Source _____

Yarn _____

Color / dye lot _____

_____

Weight _____

WPI _____

Fiber _____

Hook Size _____

Gauge _____

Washing Instructions

_____

_____

_____

_____

_____

Notes _____

_____

_____

_____

_____

Rating ☆ ☆ ☆ ☆ ☆    Difficulty ▢ ▢ ▢ ▢ ▢ ▢

Sketch ✂

27 Project Name .................................................................................................

For ..................................................  Occasion ..................................................

Start Date ..................................................  End Date ..................................................

Pattern ..................................................

Design Source ..................................................

Yarn ..................................................

Color / dye lot ..................................................

..................................................

Weight ..................................................

WPI ..................................................

Fiber ..................................................

Hook Size ..................................................

Gauge ..................................................

Washing Instructions

Notes ..................................................

Rating ☆ ☆ ☆ ☆ ☆          Difficulty ☐ ☐ ☐ ☐ ☐ ☐

Sketch ✂

**28** Project Name ........................................................

For ........................................ Occasion ........................................

Start Date ........................................ End Date ........................................

Pattern ........................................

Design Source ........................................

Yarn ........................................

Color / dye lot ........................................

........................................

Weight ........................................

WPI ........................................

Fiber ........................................

Hook Size ........................................

Gauge ........................................

Washing Instructions

........................................

........................................

........................................

........................................

........................................

........................................

Notes ........................................

........................................

........................................

........................................

........................................

Rating ☆ ☆ ☆ ☆ ☆        Difficulty ☐ ☐ ☐ ☐ ☐ ☐

Sketch ✂

**29** Project Name .................................................................

For ................................... Occasion ...................................

Start Date ................................ End Date ...............................

Pattern ...........................................................................

Design Source ....................................................................

Yarn ..............................................................

Color / dye lot ..................................................

.................................................................

Weight ..........................................................

WPI .............................................................

Fiber ...........................................................

Hook Size ......................................................

Gauge ..........................................................

Washing Instructions

.................................................

.................................................

.................................................

.................................................

.................................................

Notes .............................................................................

.................................................................................

.................................................................................

.................................................................................

Rating ☆ ☆ ☆ ☆ ☆          Difficulty ☐ ☐ ☐ ☐ ☐ ☐

Sketch ✄

**30** Project Name _____

For _____ Occasion _____

Start Date _____ End Date _____

Pattern _____

Design Source _____

Yarn _____

Color / dye lot _____

_____

Weight _____

WPS _____

Fiber _____

Hook Size _____

Gauge _____

Washing Instructions

_____

_____

_____

_____

_____

_____

Notes _____

_____

_____

_____

Rating ☆ ☆ ☆ ☆ ☆ Difficulty ☐ ☐ ☐ ☐ ☐ ☐

Sketch ✂

**31** Project Name ....................................................................................................

For ........................................... Occasion .........................................

Start Date ................................... End Date .........................................

Pattern .............................................................................................

Design Source ..................................................................................

Yarn ..................................................................................

Color / dye lot ...............................................................

..............................................................................................

Weight ..........................................................................

WPI ...............................................................................

Fiber ..............................................................................

Hook Size ..................................................................

Gauge ........................................................................

Washing Instructions

..............................................

..............................................

..............................................

..............................................

..............................................

..............................................

Notes ..........................................................................................................

..............................................................................................................

..............................................................................................................

..............................................................................................................

Rating ☆ ☆ ☆ ☆ ☆          Difficulty ☐ ☐ ☐ ☐ ☐ ☐

Sketch ✂

**32** Project Name _____

For _____ Occasion _____

Start Date _____ End Date _____

Pattern _____

Design Source _____

Yarn _____

Color / dye lot _____

_____

Weight _____

WPI _____

Fiber _____

Hook Size _____

Gauge _____

Washing Instructions

_____

_____

_____

_____

_____

Notes _____

_____

_____

_____

Rating ☆☆☆☆☆　　Difficulty ☐☐☐☐☐☐

Sketch ✂

**33** Project Name ....................................................................................

For ..................................... Occasion ...........................................

Start Date ........................... End Date ...........................................

Pattern .....................................................................................

Design Source ..........................................................................

Yarn .......................................................................................

Color / dye lot ......................................................................

..............................................................................................

Weight ...................................................................................

WPI .......................................................................................

Fiber .....................................................................................

Hook Size ............................................................................

Gauge ...................................................................................

Washing Instructions
..............................................................................................
..............................................................................................
..............................................................................................
..............................................................................................
..............................................................................................

Notes ....................................................................................
..............................................................................................
..............................................................................................
..............................................................................................
..............................................................................................

Rating ☆☆☆☆☆     Difficulty ▢▢▢▢▢▢

Sketch ✂

**34** Project Name _____

For _____ Occasion _____

Start Date _____ End Date _____

Pattern _____

Design Source _____

Yarn _____

Color / dye lot _____

_____

Weight _____

WPI _____

Fiber _____

Hook Size _____

Gauge _____

Washing Instructions

_____

_____

_____

_____

_____

Notes _____

_____

_____

_____

Rating ☆ ☆ ☆ ☆ ☆          Difficulty ▢ ▢ ▢ ▢ ▢ ▢

Sketch ✂

**35** Project Name _____

For _____ Occasion _____

Start Date _____ End Date _____

Pattern _____

Design Source _____

Yarn _____

Color / dye lot _____

_____

Weight _____

WPI _____

Fiber _____

Hook Size _____

Gauge _____

Washing Instructions

_____

_____

_____

_____

_____

Notes _____

_____

_____

_____

Rating ☆☆☆☆☆ Difficulty ▢▢▢▢▢▢

Sketch ✄

**36** Project Name ...................................................................

For .................................... Occasion ....................................

Start Date .................................... End Date ....................................

Pattern ....................................

Design Source ....................................

Yarn ....................................

Color / dye lot ....................................

....................................

Weight ....................................

WPI ....................................

Fiber ....................................

Hook Size ....................................

Gauge ....................................

Washing Instructions

....................................

....................................

....................................

....................................

Notes ....................................

....................................

....................................

....................................

Rating ☆☆☆☆☆  Difficulty ☐ ☐ ☐ ☐ ☐ ☐

Sketch ✂

**37** Project Name _____

For _____ Occasion _____

Start Date _____ End Date _____

Pattern _____

Design Source _____

Yarn _____

Color / dye lot _____

_____

Weight _____

WPI _____

Fiber _____

Hook Size _____

Gauge _____

Washing Instructions

_____

_____

_____

_____

_____

Notes _____

_____

_____

_____

Rating ☆☆☆☆☆ Difficulty ▢ ▢ ▢ ▢ ▢ ▢

Sketch ✂

**38**

Project Name .................................................

For ........................... Occasion ...........................

Start Date ........................... End Date ...........................

Pattern ...................................................

Design Source ...............................................

Yarn ...................................................

Color / dye lot ...............................................

...................................................

Weight ...................................................

WPI ...................................................

Fiber ...................................................

Hook Size ...................................................

Gauge ...................................................

Washing Instructions

...................................................

...................................................

...................................................

...................................................

...................................................

Notes ...................................................

...................................................

...................................................

...................................................

Rating ☆ ☆ ☆ ☆ ☆          Difficulty ☐ ☐ ☐ ☐ ☐ ☐

Sketch ✂

**39** Project Name

For _____ Occasion _____

Start Date _____ End Date _____

Pattern _____

Design Source _____

Yarn _____

Color / dye lot _____

_____

Weight _____

WPI _____

Fiber _____

Hook Size _____

Gauge _____

Washing Instructions

_____

_____

_____

_____

_____

Notes _____

_____

_____

_____

Rating ☆☆☆☆☆ Difficulty ☐ ☐ ☐ ☐ ☐ ☐

Sketch ✂

**40** Project Name _____

For _____ Occasion _____

Start Date _____ End Date _____

Pattern _____

Design Source _____

Yarn _____

Color / dye lot _____

_____

Weight _____

WPI _____

Fiber _____

Hook Size _____

Gauge _____

Washing Instructions

_____

_____

_____

_____

_____

Notes _____

_____

_____

_____

Rating ☆☆☆☆☆        Difficulty ▢ ▢ ▢ ▢ ▢ ▢

Sketch ✂

**41** Project Name ................................................................

For ........................................... Occasion ...........................................

Start Date ........................................... End Date ...........................................

Pattern ...........................................

Design Source ...........................................

Yarn ...........................................

Color / dye lot ...........................................

...........................................

Weight ...........................................

WPI ...........................................

Fiber ...........................................

Hook Size ...........................................

Gauge ...........................................

Washing Instructions

...........................................

...........................................

...........................................

...........................................

...........................................

Notes ...........................................

...........................................

...........................................

...........................................

Rating ☆ ☆ ☆ ☆ ☆          Difficulty ☐ ☐ ☐ ☐ ☐ ☐

Sketch ✂

**42** Project Name _____

For _____ Occasion _____

Start Date _____ End Date _____

Pattern _____

Design Source _____

Yarn _____

Color / dye lot _____

_____

Weight _____

WPI _____

Fiber _____

Hook Size _____

Gauge _____

Washing Instructions

_____
_____
_____
_____
_____
_____
_____

Notes _____
_____
_____
_____
_____

Rating ☆☆☆☆☆    Difficulty ☐ ☐ ☐ ☐ ☐ ☐

Sketch ✂

**43** Project Name _____

For _____ Occasion _____

Start Date _____ End Date _____

Pattern _____

Design Source _____

Yarn _____

Color / dye lot _____

_____

Weight _____

WPI _____

Fiber _____

Hook Size _____

Gauge _____

Washing Instructions

_____

_____

_____

_____

_____

Notes _____

_____

_____

_____

Rating ☆☆☆☆☆        Difficulty ▢ ▢ ▢ ▢ ▢ ▢

Sketch ✂

**44** Project Name ...................................................

For ................................. Occasion .................................

Start Date ......................... End Date .........................

Pattern ...................................................

Design Source ...................................................

Yarn ...................................................

Color / dye lot ...................................................

...................................................

Weight ...................................................

WPI ...................................................

Fiber ...................................................

Hook Size ...................................................

Gauge ...................................................

Washing Instructions

...................................................

...................................................

...................................................

...................................................

...................................................

Notes ...................................................

...................................................

...................................................

...................................................

Rating ☆ ☆ ☆ ☆ ☆          Difficulty ▢ ▢ ▢ ▢ ▢ ▢

Sketch ✄

**45** Project Name ............................................

For .................................... Occasion ....................................

Start Date .................................... End Date ....................................

Pattern ....................................

Design Source ....................................

Yarn ....................................

Color / dye lot ....................................

....................................

Weight ....................................

WPI ....................................

Fiber ....................................

Hook Size ....................................

Gauge ....................................

Washing Instructions

....................................

....................................

....................................

....................................

....................................

Notes ....................................

....................................

....................................

....................................

Rating ☆ ☆ ☆ ☆ ☆      Difficulty ☐ ☐ ☐ ☐ ☐ ☐

Sketch ✂

**46**

Project Name ......................................................

For ............................................ Occasion ..................................

Start Date ....................................... End Date ...............................

Pattern ...........................................................

Design Source .......................................................

Yarn ...........................................................

Color / dye lot ........................................

..............................................................

Weight .......................................................

WPI ..........................................................

Fiber ........................................................

Hook Size ....................................................

Gauge ........................................................

Washing Instructions

..............................................................
..............................................................
..............................................................
..............................................................
..............................................................
..............................................................

Notes ...........................................................
..............................................................
..............................................................
..............................................................
..............................................................

Rating ☆ ☆ ☆ ☆ ☆          Difficulty ☐ ☐ ☐ ☐ ☐ ☐

Sketch ✂

**47** Project Name ........................................................

For ........................................ Occasion ........................................

Start Date ........................................ End Date ........................................

Pattern ........................................................

Design Source ........................................................

Yarn ........................................................

Color / dye lot ........................................

........................................................

Weight ........................................

WPI ........................................

Fiber ........................................

Hook Size ........................................

Gauge ........................................

Washing Instructions

........................................................

........................................................

........................................................

........................................................

........................................................

Notes ........................................................

........................................................

........................................................

........................................................

Rating ☆ ☆ ☆ ☆ ☆          Difficulty ▢ ▢ ▢ ▢ ▢ ▢

Sketch ✄

**48** Project Name ............................................................

For ........................... Occasion ...........................

Start Date ........................... End Date ...........................

Pattern ...........................

Design Source ...........................

Yarn ...........................

Color / dye lot ...........................

...........................

Weight ...........................

WPI ...........................

Fiber ...........................

Hook Size ...........................

Gauge ...........................

Washing Instructions
...........................
...........................
...........................
...........................
...........................

Notes ...........................
...........................
...........................
...........................

Rating ☆ ☆ ☆ ☆ ☆    Difficulty ☐ ☐ ☐ ☐ ☐ ☐

Sketch ✂

**49** Project Name ....................................................

For .................................... Occasion ....................................

Start Date .................................... End Date ....................................

Pattern ....................................................

Design Source ....................................................

Yarn ....................................................

Color / dye lot ....................................

....................................................

Weight ....................................

WPI ....................................

Fiber ....................................

Hook Size ....................................

Gauge ....................................

Washing Instructions

....................................................

....................................................

....................................................

....................................................

....................................................

Notes ....................................................

....................................................

....................................................

....................................................

Rating ☆ ☆ ☆ ☆ ☆          Difficulty ☐ ☐ ☐ ☐ ☐ ☐

Sketch ✂

**50** Project Name _____

For _____ Occasion _____

Start Date _____ End Date _____

Pattern _____

Design Source _____

Yarn _____

Color / dye lot _____

_____

Weight _____

WPI _____

Fiber _____

Hook Size _____

Gauge _____

Washing Instructions

_____

_____

_____

_____

_____

_____

Notes _____

_____

_____

_____

Rating ☆☆☆☆☆ Difficulty ☐ ☐ ☐ ☐ ☐ ☐

Sketch ✂

**51** Project Name

For ............................ Occasion ............................

Start Date ............................ End Date ............................

Pattern ............................

Design Source ............................

Yarn ............................

Color / dye lot ............................

............................

Weight ............................

WPI ............................

Fiber ............................

Hook Size ............................

Gauge ............................

Washing Instructions

............................

............................

............................

............................

............................

Notes ............................

............................

............................

............................

............................

Rating ☆ ☆ ☆ ☆ ☆          Difficulty ▢ ▢ ▢ ▢ ▢ ▢

Sketch ✂

**52** Project Name _____

For _____ Occasion _____

Start Date _____ End Date _____

Pattern _____

Design Source _____

Yarn _____

Color / dye lot _____

_____

Weight _____

WPI _____

Fiber _____

Hook Size _____

Gauge _____

Washing Instructions
_____
_____
_____
_____
_____
_____

Notes _____
_____
_____
_____
_____

Rating ☆ ☆ ☆ ☆ ☆         Difficulty ☐ ☐ ☐ ☐ ☐ ☐

112

Sketch ✂

**53** Project Name _____

For _____ Occasion _____

Start Date _____ End Date _____

Pattern _____

Design Source _____

Yarn _____

Color / dye lot _____

_____

Weight _____

WPI _____

Fiber _____

Hook Size _____

Gauge _____

Washing Instructions

_____

_____

_____

_____

_____

Notes _____

_____

_____

_____

Rating ☆☆☆☆☆ Difficulty ☐☐☐☐☐☐

Sketch ✂

**54**

Project Name ..............................................................

For ........................................... Occasion ...........................................

Start Date ........................................... End Date ...........................................

Pattern ..............................................................

Design Source ..............................................................

Yarn ..............................................................

Color / dye lot ..............................................................

..............................................................

Weight ..............................................................

WPI ..............................................................

Fiber ..............................................................

Hook Size ..............................................................

Gauge ..............................................................

Washing Instructions

..............................................................

..............................................................

..............................................................

..............................................................

..............................................................

..............................................................

Notes ..............................................................

..............................................................

..............................................................

..............................................................

..............................................................

Rating ☆☆☆☆☆ Difficulty ▢ ▢ ▢ ▢ ▢ ▢

Sketch ✂

**55** Project Name _____

For _____ Occasion _____

Start Date _____ End Date _____

Pattern _____

Design Source _____

Yarn _____

Color / dye lot _____

_____

Weight _____

WPI _____

Fiber _____

Hook Size _____

Gauge _____

Washing Instructions

_____

_____

_____

_____

_____

Notes _____

_____

_____

_____

Rating ☆☆☆☆☆ Difficulty ☐ ☐ ☐ ☐ ☐ ☐

Sketch

**56** Project Name .................................................

For .................................. Occasion ..................................

Start Date .............................. End Date ..............................

Pattern ....................................................................

Design Source ..............................................................

Yarn ....................................................................

Color / dye lot ..........................................................

..............................................................................

Weight ..................................................................

WPI ....................................................................

Fiber ..................................................................

Hook Size ..............................................................

Gauge ..................................................................

Washing Instructions

..............................................................................

..............................................................................

..............................................................................

..............................................................................

..............................................................................

..............................................................................

..............................................................................

Notes ..................................................................

..............................................................................

..............................................................................

..............................................................................

..............................................................................

Rating ☆ ☆ ☆ ☆ ☆    Difficulty ☐ ☐ ☐ ☐ ☐ ☐

Sketch ✂

**57** Project Name ........................................................

For ................................ Occasion ................................

Start Date ................................ End Date ................................

Pattern ................................................

Design Source ................................................

Yarn ................................................

Color / dye lot ................................................

................................................

Weight ................................................

WPI ................................................

Fiber ................................................

Hook Size ................................................

Gauge ................................................

Washing Instructions

................................................

................................................

................................................

Notes ................................................

................................................

................................................

................................................

Rating ☆ ☆ ☆ ☆ ☆     Difficulty ☐ ☐ ☐ ☐ ☐ ☐

Sketch ✂

**58** Project Name ............................................................

For ........................................... Occasion ...........................................

Start Date ........................................... End Date ...........................................

Pattern ...........................................

Design Source ...........................................

Yarn ...........................................

Color / dye lot ...........................................

...........................................

Weight ...........................................

WPI ...........................................

Fiber ...........................................

Hook Size ...........................................

Gauge ...........................................

Washing Instructions

...........................................

...........................................

...........................................

...........................................

Notes ...........................................

...........................................

...........................................

...........................................

Rating ☆ ☆ ☆ ☆ ☆          Difficulty ☐ ☐ ☐ ☐ ☐ ☐

Sketch ✂

**59** Project Name _____

For _____ Occasion _____

Start Date _____ End Date _____

Pattern _____

Design Source _____

Yarn _____

Color / dye lot _____

_____

Weight _____

WPI _____

Fiber _____

Hook Size _____

Gauge _____

Washing Instructions _____

_____

_____

_____

Notes _____

_____

_____

_____

Rating ☆ ☆ ☆ ☆ ☆    Difficulty ☐ ☐ ☐ ☐ ☐ ☐

Sketch ✂

**60** Project Name ...............................................

For ............................... Occasion ...............................

Start Date ............................... End Date ...............................

Pattern ...............................................

Design Source ...............................................

Yarn ...............................................

Color / dye lot ...............................................

...............................................

Weight ...............................................

WPI ...............................................

Fiber ...............................................

Hook Size ...............................................

Gauge ...............................................

Washing Instructions

...............................................

...............................................

...............................................

...............................................

...............................................

Notes ...............................................

...............................................

...............................................

...............................................

Rating ☆ ☆ ☆ ☆ ☆          Difficulty ☐ ☐ ☐ ☐ ☐ ☐

Sketch ✂

**61** Project Name ......................................................

For ....................................... Occasion ...............................

Start Date ............................. End Date ..............................

Pattern .............................................................

Design Source ..................................................

Yarn ..............................................................

Color / dye lot ................................................

.........................................................................

Weight ...........................................................

WPI ..................................................................

Fiber ..............................................................

Hook Size .......................................................

Gauge ............................................................

Washing Instructions

.........................................................................

.........................................................................

.........................................................................

.........................................................................

.........................................................................

Notes ...............................................................

.........................................................................

.........................................................................

.........................................................................

.........................................................................

Rating ☆ ☆ ☆ ☆ ☆     Difficulty ☐ ☐ ☐ ☐ ☐ ☐

Sketch ✂

**62** Project Name _____

For _____ Occasion _____

Start Date _____ End Date _____

Pattern _____

Design Source _____

Yarn _____

Color / dye lot _____

_____

Weight _____

WPI _____

Fiber _____

Hook Size _____

Gauge _____

Washing Instructions

_____

_____

_____

_____

_____

Notes _____

_____

_____

_____

Rating ☆ ☆ ☆ ☆ ☆    Difficulty ☐ ☐ ☐ ☐ ☐ ◯

Sketch ✂

**63** Project Name ..................

For .................... Occasion ....................

Start Date .................... End Date ....................

Pattern ....................

Design Source ....................

Yarn ....................

Color / dye lot ....................

....................

Weight ....................

WPI ....................

Fiber ....................

Hook Size ....................

Gauge ....................

Washing Instructions

....................

....................

....................

....................

....................

Notes ....................

....................

....................

....................

Rating ☆ ☆ ☆ ☆ ☆   Difficulty ☐ ☐ ☐ ☐ ☐ ☐

Sketch ✂

**64** Project Name ...................................................

For ........................................ Occasion .................................

Start Date ................................ End Date ................................

Pattern .................................................................

Design Source .........................................................

Yarn ...................................................

Color / dye lot .........................................................

.........................................................

Weight .........................................................

WPI .........................................................

Fiber .........................................................

Hook Size .........................................................

Gauge .........................................................

Washing Instructions

.........................................................

.........................................................

.........................................................

.........................................................

.........................................................

Notes .........................................................

.........................................................

.........................................................

.........................................................

.........................................................

Rating ☆ ☆ ☆ ☆ ☆        Difficulty ☐ ☐ ☐ ☐ ☐ ☐

Sketch ✂

Made in the USA
Monee, IL
09 January 2025